Home Maid

Spanish

Home Maid Spanish Series

Home Maid Spanish
MARGARET STORM and ELSIE GINNETT

Home Maid Spanish Cookbook
MARGARET STORM and ELSIE GINNETT

Home Maid

Spanish

MARGARET STORM and ELSIE GINNETT

Crown Publishers, Inc.
New York

Revised and enlarged edition

Library of Congress Cataloging-in-Publication Data
Storm, Margaret. Home maid Spanish.
1.   Spanish language—Conversation and phrase
books (for servants)   I.   Ginnett, Elsie B., joint
author.   II.   Title.
PC4120.S45S8   1976   468'.3'421024635   76-11825
ISBN 0-517-535106

Design and illustration by Barbara Monahan
Logo adapted from illustration by Winona J. Hawken

20   19   18   17   16   15

Contents

Spanish Alphabet Pronunciation

A   The A is pronounced as "a" in "father."

E   The E is pronounced as "e" in "best."

I   The I is pronounced as "ee" in "beet."

O   The O is pronounced as "o" in "north."

U   The U is pronounced as "oo" in "tool."

B   The B is pronounced as "b" in "bit."

C   The C before a, o, or u is hard as the "c" in "can."
The C before e or i is soft as the "c" in "cent."

CC   The CC is pronounced "kx." "Acción" is pronounced "akxion."

CH   The CH is pronounced as "ch" in "children."

D   The D is pronounced as "d" in "dog."

G   The G before a, o, or u is hard as the "g" in "got."
The G before e or i is pronounced as "h" in "hen."

H   The H is always silent in Spanish.

J   The J is pronounced as "h" in "hen."

L   The L is pronounced as "l" in "letter."

LL   The LL is pronounced as "y" in "yet."

Ñ   The Ñ is pronounced as "ny" in "canyon."
"Señor" is pronounced "senyor."

QU   The QU is pronounced as "k" in "kangaroo."

RR   The RR is strongly trilled.

T   The T is pronounced as "tt" in "attract."

X   The X is pronounced as "xe" in "xerox."

Y   The Y is pronounced as "y" in "yet."
When the letter Y stands alone, it is pronounced as "ee" in "beet."

Z   The Z is pronounced as "s" in "sent."

Concerning the position of the accent in Spanish, all words ending in a vowel, n, or s have the accent on the next to last syllable. In all other cases, the accent is on the last syllable unless it is marked by an accent.

F, K, M, N, P, R, S, U, and V are pronounced as in English.

Days of the Week
Los Días de la Semana

Monday	*Lunes*	Friday	*Viernes*
Tuesday	*Martes*	Saturday	*Sábado*
Wednesday	*Miércoles*	Sunday	*Domingo*
Thursday	*Jueves*		

Months of the Year
Los Meses del Año

January	*Enero*	July	*Julio*
February	*Febrero*	August	*Agosto*
March	*Marzo*	September	*Septiembre*
April	*Abril*	October	*Octubre*
May	*Mayo*	November	*Noviembre*
June	*Junio*	December	*Diciembre*

Seasons
Las Estaciones

spring	*la primavera*	autumn	*el otoño*
summer	*el verano*	winter	*el invierno*

Colors
Los Colores

black	*negro*	orange	*naranjo*
blue	*azul*	purple	*morado*
brown	*moreno*	red	*rojo*
gray	*gris*	white	*blanco*
green	*verde*	yellow	*amarillo*

Numbers
Los Números

Cardinal
Cardinales

one	*uno*	sixteen	*diez y seis*
two	*dos*	seventeen	*diez y siete*
three	*tres*	eighteen	*diez y ocho*
four	*cuatro*	nineteen	*diez y nueve*
five	*cinco*	twenty	*veinte*
six	*seis*	thirty	*treinta*
seven	*siete*	forty	*cuarenta*
eight	*ocho*	fifty	*cincuenta*
nine	*nueve*	sixty	*sesenta*
ten	*diez*	seventy	*setenta*
eleven	*once*	eighty	*ochenta*
twelve	*doce*	ninety	*noventa*
thirteen	*trece*	hundred	*ciento*
fourteen	*catorce*	five hundred	*quinientos*
fifteen	*quince*	thousand	*mil*

Ordinal
Ordinales

first	*primero*	sixth	*sexto*
second	*segundo*	seventh	*séptimo*
third	*tercero*	eighth	*octavo*
fourth	*cuarto*	ninth	*noveno*
fifth	*quinto*	tenth	*décimo*

Holidays
Las Fiestas

Commonly Celebrated in the United States
Comunmente Celebradas en los Estados Unidos

Birthday	*Cumpleaños*
New Year's Day, 1 January	*El Primer Día del Año, 1 Enero*
Lent	*La Cuaresma*
Easter	*Pascua Florida*
Independence Day, 4 July	*Día de Independencia, 4 Julio*
Labor Day	*Día de Trabajo*
Yom Kippur	*Yom Kippur*
Hanukkah	*Hanukkah*
Thanksgiving	*Día de Gracias*
Christmas, 25 December	*La Navidad, 25 Diciembre*

Mexican National
Mexicanas Nacionales

Intervention of the French 1862, led by Ignacio Zaragoza, 5 May	*Intervención Francesa 1862 dirigida por Ignacio Zaragoza, 5 Mayo*
War for Independence, led by Father Hidalgo, 16 September	*Guerra de la Independencia dirigida por el Padre Hidalgo, 16 Septiembre*
All Saints' Day, 1 November	*Día de Todos Santos, 1 Noviembre*
Day of Virgin of Guadalupe patron saint of Mexico, 12 December	*Día de la Virgen de Guadalupe patrona de México, 12 Diciembre*

Everyday Expressions
Expresiones Diarias

Good morning	*Buenos días*
Good afternoon	*Buenas tardes*
Good evening	*Buenas noches*
Good night	*Buenas noches*
Goodbye	*Adiós*
Thank you	*Muchas gracias*
You're welcome.	*De nada.*
	Por nada.
Excuse me.	*Perdóneme.*
	Dispénseme.
Please	*Por favor*
Speak more slowly.	*Hable más despacio.*
I don't understand.	*No entiendo.*
How do you do?	*Cómo le va?*
I am sorry.	*Lo siento.*

First Day
El Primer Día

What is your name?
Cómo se llama usted?

My name is _____.
Mi nombre es _____.

Where do you live?
Dónde vive usted?

What is your address?
Qué es su dirección?

Do you have a telephone? What is the number?
Tiene usted teléfono? Qué es el número?

_____ will be your day off.
_____ sera su dia de descanso.

Will you live in?
Quiere usted vivir aqui conmigo?

Your day's work will start at _____.
Usted empieza a trabajar a las _____.

Your day's work will end at _____.
Usted termina de trabajar a las _____.

I will furnish your uniforms.
Yo tengo uniformes para usted.

Please furnish your own uniforms.
Usted tiene que traer sus uniformes.

This is your room. Make yourself at home.
Este es su cuarto. Mi casa es suya.

You may use this room in order to change your clothes.
Usted puede usar este cuarto para cambiar la ropa.

You may hang your clothes in this closet.
Usted puede colgar la ropa en este ropero.

This is your key to the door.
Esta es su llave para la puerta.

The nearest Catholic Church is located at _____.
La iglesia Catolica mas cerca esta en _____.

You will not work on these holidays: 4th of July, Labor
Day, Thanksgiving, Christmas, New Year's Day.
Usted no trabaja en éstos dias de fiesta: el 4 de Julio, el Dia del
Trabajo (es el primer lunes de Septiembre), el Dia de Gracias, La
Navidad, Día del Año Nuevo.

What Mexican or Church holidays do you observe?
Cuáles días de fiesta observa usted?

If you hurt yourself while working, please let me know
immediately.
Si se hiere cuando está trabajando, avíseme en seguida.

La Sala

las cortinas

la lámpara

los cuadros

las flores
el florero

el fogón

las almohadas
el sofá

la mesa de café

el tapete

la silla

la alfombra

Living Room
La Sala

Please clean the living room.
Limpie la sala, por favor.

Vacuum the carpet or rug.
Limpie la alfombra con la aspiradora.

Vacuum the drapes and the furniture.
Limpie las cortinas y los muebles con la aspiradora.

Move the furniture and vacuum behind it.
Mueva los muebles y limpie detrás.

Dust the furniture. Dust the pictures.
Quite el polvo de los muebles. Quite el polvo de los cuadros.

Dust the books and bookcase, but do not use the oiled cloth on the books.
Quite el polvo de los libros y del estante pero no use el paño encerado para los libros.

Wax and polish the furniture.
Encere y saque brillo a los muebles.

Wax and polish the piano, but do not wax the keys.
Encere y saque brillo al piano pero no encere las teclas.

Wax and polish the floor.
Encere y saque brillo al piso.

Wash the windows. Wash the curtains. Wash the ashtrays.
Lave las ventanas. Lave las cortinas. Lave los ceniceros.

Clean the fireplace, fire screen, and andirons.
Limpie el fogón, el alambrado y los utensilios.

Empty the ashes from the fireplace.
Vacíe las cenizas del fogón.

This is very valuable. Please be careful when you handle it.
Este es muy valioso, por favor, tenga mucho cuidado con ello.

Put the mail on this table.
Ponga la correspondencia en esta mesa.

La Recámara

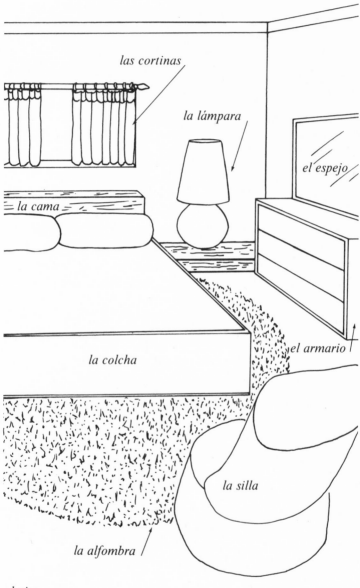

las cortinas

la lámpara

el espejo

la cama

la colcha

el armario

la silla

la alfombra

el piso

Bedroom
La Recámara

Please clean the bedroom.
Limpie la recámara, por favor.

Make the bed.
Tienda la cama.

Change the sheets and pillowcases.
Cambie las sábanas y las fundas.

Dust the bureau, dressing table, and chest of drawers.
Quite el polvo del bufete, del tocador, y del armario.

Clean and polish the mirrors.
Limpie y saque brillo a los espejos.

Clean the closets.
Limpie los roperos.

Vacuum the carpet.
Limpie la alfombra con la aspiradora.

Wax and polish the floor.
Encere y saque brillo al piso.

Vacuum the drapes.
Limpie las cortinas con la aspiradora.

Wash the curtains.
Lave las cortinas.

Wash the windows.
Lave las ventanas.

Wash the blankets.
Lave las cobijas.

Turn the mattress.
Dele la vuelta al colchon.

La Cocina

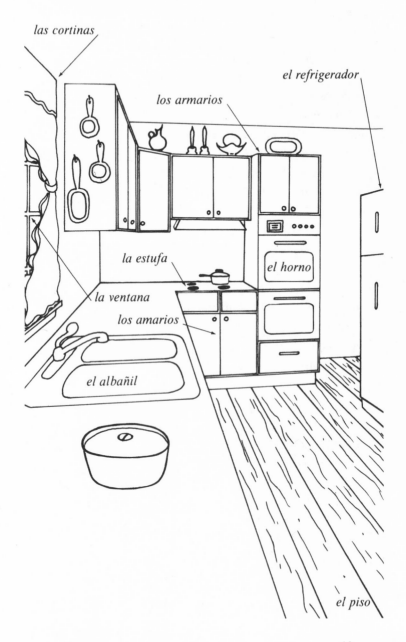

las cortinas

el refrigerador

los armarios

la estufa

el horno

la ventana

los amarios

el albañil

el piso

Kitchen
La Cocina

Sweep the kitchen floor.
Barra el piso de la cocina.

Scrub the kitchen floor.
Restriegue el piso de la cocina.

Wax and polish the kitchen floor.
Encere y saque brillo al el piso de la cocina.

Clean the stove, the oven, and the burners on top.
Limpie la estufa, el horno, y las parrillas.

Wash the refrigerator inside and outside; wash the shelves.
Lave el refrigerador por dentro y por fuera; lave las repisas.

Defrost the refrigerator by turning the dial to _____.
Descongele el refrigerador dándole vuelta al medidor a _____.

Reset the refrigerator by turning the dial to _____.
Ponga en marcha el refrigerador dándole vuelta al medidor a
_____.

Wash the cupboards inside and outside. Change the shelf
paper.
*Lave los armarios por dentro y por fuera. Cambie el papel en las
repisas.*

Clean and scour the sink and counter.
Limpie y estregue el albañal y el tablero de la cocina.

Empty the wastebasket into the trash container in the yard.
Vacíe el cesto en el bote de basura afuera.

Empty the garbage into the large garbage can in the yard.
Vacíe los desperdicios en el bote de basura en el patio.

Wrap the garbage in newspaper.
Envuelva los desperdicios en el periódico.

Scrub the garbage can and then rinse it.
Lave el bote de basura y enjuáguelo.

Polish the silver.
Saque brillo a los cubiertos.

We like breakfast served at _____.
Nos gusta que nos sirva el desayuno a las _____.

We like lunch served at _____.
Nos gusta que nos sirva el almuerzo a las _____.

We like dinner served at _____.
Nos gusta que nos sirva la cena a las _____.

Will you cook a Mexican dinner for us sometime?
Cocinaría usted una comida mexicana para nosotros alguna vez?

Have you ever shopped in a supermarket?
Ha ido usted al supermercado?

I will shop with you today.
Yo iré con usted hoy al mercado.

Do you know how to make change in American money?
Sabe usted cambiar el dinero americano?

Put the groceries away.
Ponga los comestibles en el armario.

Wash the lettuce and greens thoroughly before you put them away.
Lave la lechuga y las verduras bien antes de ponerlas en el refrigerador.

Put these in the freezer.
Ponga ésto en el congelador.

The canned food goes here.
Las comidas enlatadas deben de estar aquí.

Store this here.
Ponga ésto aquí.

Use this dishpan and soap for the dishes.
Use este sartén y jabón para los trastos.

Rinse the dishes in hot water.
Enjuague los trastos en agua caliente.

Set them to drain in this rack.
Póngalos que se estilen en este estilador.

This is the automatic dishwasher.
Este es el lavaplatos.

Scrape plates carefully.
Limpie los platos cuidadosamente.

Rinse the dishes well and set them in racks in the machine.
Enjuáguelos bien, póngalos en los espacios de la máquina.

Add this special cleaner.
Añada este jabón especial.

Turn on the machine like this.
Ponga en marcha la máquina de esta manera.

El Cuarto de Baño

el techo

la cortina del baño

el espejo

las cortinas

la regadera

las toallas

las llaves
de agua

el lavamanos

el escusado

el mosaico

el baño

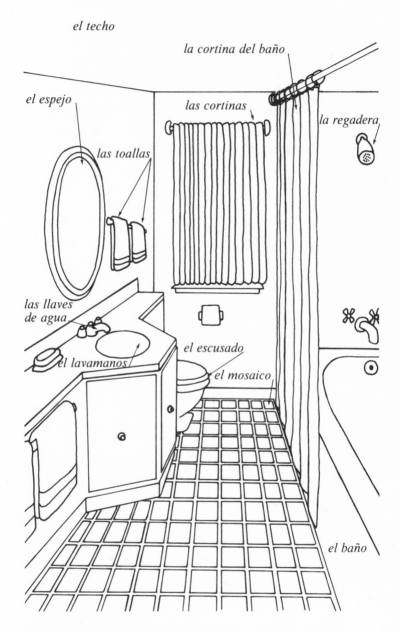

Bathroom
El Cuarto de Baño

Please clean the bathroom floor.
Por favor, limpie el piso del cuarto de baño.

Please sweep the bathroom floor.
Por favor, barra el piso del cuarto de baño.

Please scrub the bathroom floor.
Por favor, estregue el piso del cuarto de baño.

Clean the toilet inside and outside.
Limpie el escusado por dentro y afuera.

Scour the toilet inside and outside.
Friegue el escusado por dentro y afuera.

This is the brush for the toilet.
Este es el cepillo para el escusado.

Scour the bathtub and wash bowl.
Friegue el baño y el lavamanos.

Polish the fixtures.
Saque brillo a las llaves de agua.

Please wash and polish the mirror.
Lave y saque brillo al espejo.

Empty the hamper and take the clothes to the laundry room.
Vacie el costillo y lleve la ropa al cuarto donde se lavan.

Wash the shower walls.
Lave las paredes del baño.

Wash the floor of the shower.
Lave el piso del baño.

Wash the shower curtain.
Lave la cortina del baño.

Wash and polish the glass of the shower door.
Lave y saque brillo al vidrio del baño.

La Ropa Para Lavar

la pared

el detergente

decolorante

el estante

la máquina para lavar

el secador

la tabla de planchar

la plancha

el cesto

Laundry
La Ropa Para Lavar

Sprinkle the clothes. Iron the clothes. Iron the sheets.
Rocíe la ropa. Planche la ropa. Planche las sábanas.

Please wash the clothes.
Por favor, lave la ropa.

Separate the white from the colored clothes.
Separe la ropa blanca de la ropa de color.

Wash nylon underwear separately (by hand).
Lave la ropa íntima a mano.

Bleach these clothes.
Blanquee ésta ropa.

Starch these clothes. Starch the collars and cuffs of the shirts.
Almidone esta ropa. Almidone el cuello y los puños de las camisas.

Put clothes in the dryer.
Ponga la ropa en el secador.

Hang the clothes on the line. Here are the clothes pins.
Tienda la ropa en el tendedero. Aquí están las pinzas.

Fold towels and wash cloths.
Doble las toallas y paños de lavar.

Give these clothes to the man from the cleaners when he comes.
De esta ropa al señor de la tintorería cuando venga.

This bundle of laundry will be called for by the man from the laundry.
El señor de la tintorería vendrá por este lío.

This is the linen closet; put sheets and pillowcases here.
Este es el armario para el lino; ponga las sábanas y las fundas aquí.

Put towels on this shelf.
Ponga las toallas en esta repisa.

Keep it neat, please.
Manténgalo bien arreglado.

El Cuarto de la Familia

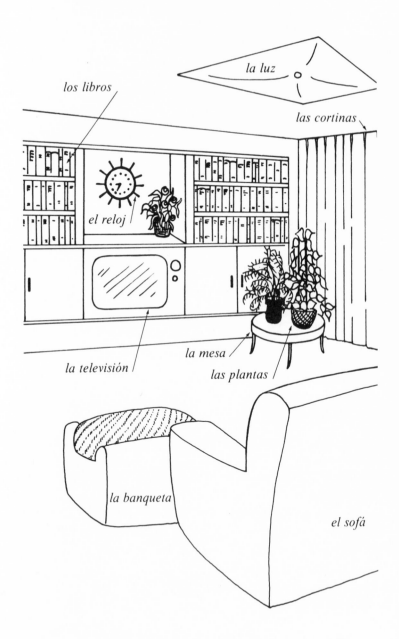

la luz

los libros

las cortinas

el reloj

la televisión

la mesa

las plantas

la banqueta

el sofá

Family Room
El Cuarto de la Familia

Please clean the family room.
Por favor, limpie el cuarto de la familia.

Vacuum the carpet.
Limpie la alfombra con la aspiradora.

Dust the television set.
Quite el polvo de la televisión.

Dust, wax, and polish the desk, but do not disturb papers on top.
Quite el polvo, encere, y saque brillo al escritorio, pero no mueva los papeles de encima.

Empty the ashtrays.
Vacíe los ceniceros.

Empty the wastebasket.
Vacíe el cesto.

Pick up the children's toys and place them on the shelves in this box.
Recoja los juguetes de los niños y póngalos en las repisas en esta caja.

Put magazines on this shelf.
Ponga las revistas en esta repisa.

Dispose of newspapers—put them in the garage.
Disponga de los periódicos—póngalos en el garage.

Dispose of newspapers—put them on the back porch.
Disponga de los periódicos—póngalos en el pórtico.

Dispose of newspapers—put them in the trash.
Disponga de los periódicos—póngalos en el bote de basura.

El Cuidado de los Niños

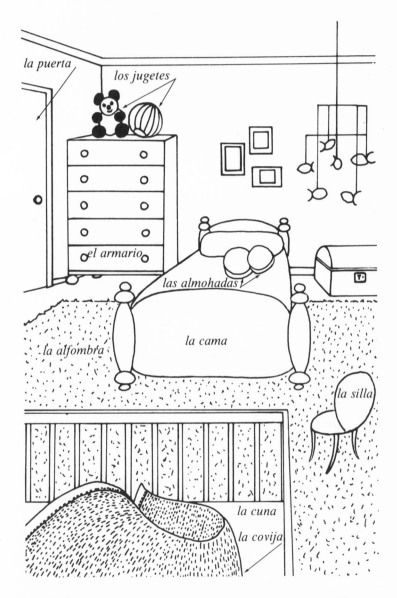

la puerta

los jugetes

el armario

las almohadas

la cama

la alfombra

la silla

la cuna

la covija

Child Care
El Cuidado de los Niños

The baby's name is _____.
El nombre del niño es _____.

My daughter's name is _____.
El nombre de mi hija es _____.

My son's name is _____.
El nombre de mi hijo es _____.

The clean diapers are kept here.
Los pañales limpios se guardan aquí.

Put the soiled diapers here.
Ponga los pañales sucios aquí.

These are disposable diapers.
Estos son pañales disponibles.

Feed the baby at _____.
Dé de comer al niño a las _____.

Heat the bottle.
Caliente la botella.

Give the baby soup, vegetable, fruit, egg, and orange juice.
Dé al niño sopa, legumbre, fruta, huevo, y jugo de naranja.

Nap time is _____.
La hora de siesta es a las _____.

The children will be home from school at _____.
Los niños vienen de la escuela a las _____.

Give the children their lunch at _____.
Sirva el almuerzo a los niños a las _____.

Give the children cookies and milk after school.
Después de que vengan de la escuela, dé a los niños bollos y leche.

Make sure the children change their clothes before they go out to play.
Asegúrese de que los niños cambien de ropa antes de jugar.

Give the children their dinner at _____.
Dé la cena a los niños a las _____.

Put the children to bed at _____.
Los niños se acuestan a las _____.

Be sure the baby keeps covered.
Asegúrese de que el niño esté bien cobijado/cubierto.

Do not allow the children to watch television after _____.
No les permita a los niños ver la televisión después de las _____.

Give the children a bath before bedtime.
De un baño a los niños antes de que se acuesten.

Be sure the children brush their teeth before leaving for school.
Asegúrese de que los niños se laven los dientes antes de salir para la escuela.

Be sure the children brush their teeth before going to bed.
Asegúrese de que los niños se laven los dientes antes de acostarse.

If necessary, I can be reached at _____.
Si es necesario, usted puede encontrarme en _____.

The doctor's name is _____.
El médico se llama _____.

His telephone number is _____.
Su número de teléfono es _____.

Vocabulary
El Vocabulario

A

about *acerca de*

above *arriba*

address *la dirección*

adhesive tape *tela adhesiva*

afterward *después*

against *contra*

almost *casi*

although *aunque*

apartment *apartamiento*

apple *la manzana*

apricot *el chavacano*

apron *el delantal*

arm *el brazo*

arrive, to *llegar*

ashtray *el cenicero*

asparagus *los espárragos*

aspirin *aspirina*

B

back *la espalda*

bacon *el tocino*

bad *malo (a)*

bakery *la panadería*

baking powder *la levadura*

ball *la pelota*

banana *el plátano*

bandage *el vendaje*

band-aid *la curita*

barbecue *la barbacoa*

bath *el baño*

beach *la playa*

bean *el frijol*

bean, string *el ejote*

beater *el batidor*

beautiful *bello (a)*

beauty shop *el salón de belleza*

because *porque*

bed *la cama*

bedroom *la recámara*

bedspread *la colcha*

beef *la res*

beer *la cerveza*

beet *el betabel*

before *antes*

behind *detrás*

bell *la campana*

beneath *debajo*

bird *el pájaro*

birthday *el cumpleaños*

black *negro (a)*

blanket *la cobija*

bleach, to *blanquear*

blond *rubio*

bone *el hueso*

both *ambos (as)*

bottom *el fondo*

box *la caja*

brandy *coñac*

bread *el pan*

broom *la escoba*

brush *el cepillo*

bucket *balde*

burn, to *arder*

butter *la mantequilla*

buy, to *comprar*

C

cabbage *el repollo*

cake   *el pastel*
can   *la lata*
canary   *el canario*
candle   *la vela*
candy   *el dulce*
can opener   *el abrelatas*
carpet   *la alfombra*
carrot   *la zanahoria*
carry, to   *llevar*
cat   *el gato*
cauliflower   *la coliflor*
celery   *el apio*
chair   *la silla*
chandelier   *el candil*
cheap   *barato (a)*
cheese   *el queso*
cherry   *la cereza*
chest, body   *el pecho*
chicken   *el pollo*
children   *los niños*
chocolate   *el chocolate*
chops   *las chuletas*
church   *la iglesia*
cinnamon   *la canela*
clean, to   *limpiar*
cleaners   *la limpiadoría*
clock   *el reloj*
close, to   *cerrar*
closet   *el armario*
cloth   *el paño*
clothes   *la ropa*
clothes line   *el tendedero*
clothes pin   *la pinza*
coat   *el abrigo*
cocktail   *el coctel*
coffee   *el café*
cold   *frío*
collar   *el collar*
color   *el color*
comb   *el peine*

cook   *la cocinera*
cook, to   *cocer*
cookies   *los bollos*
cord   *la cuerda*
corkscrew   *el tirabuzón*
corn   *el maíz*
corner   *la esquina*
cornstarch   *la maicena*
cotton   *el algodón*
cough, to   *toser*
counter   *el tablero de la
          cocina*
cousin   *el primo (a)*
cover, to   *cubrir*
crackers   *las galletitas*
cream   *la crema*
crib   *la cuna*
crumbs   *las migajas*
cry, to   *llorar*
cuff   *el puño*
cuff links   *los yugos*
cup   *la taza*
cupboard   *el armario*
curtains   *las cortinas*
custard   *el flan*
cut, to   *cortar*

D

damp   *húmedo*
dance, to   *bailar*
dark   *obscuro*
darn, to   *zurcir*
daughter   *la hija*
daughter-in-law   *la nuera*
dessert   *el postre*
detergent   *detergente*
difficult   *difícil*
dining room   *el comedor*
dirty   *sucio (a)*
dish   *el plato*

dishwasher   *la lavadora de platos*
dog   *el perro*
dog food   *alimento para perros*
doll   *la muñeca*
door   *la puerta*
double boiler   *el baño maría*
down   *abajo*
dozen   *la docena*
drainboard   *el estilador*
drapes   *las cortinas*
drawer   *el cajón*
dream   *el sueño*
drink, to   *beber*
drugstore   *la botica*
dry, to   *secar*
dryer   *el secador*
dust   *el polvo*
dust, to   *sacudir*

E

ear   *la oreja*
early   *temprano*
earring   *el arete*
egg   *el huevo*
elastic   *el elástico*
elbow   *el codo*
empty, to   *vaciar*
end   *el cabo*
enough   *bastante*
expensive   *caro (a)*
eye   *el ojo*

F

face   *la cara*
fat   *gordo*
father   *padre*
father-in-law   *el suegro*
faucet   *la llave*

fertilizer   *el estiércol*
fig   *el higo*
fill, to   *llenar*
finger   *el dedo*
finish, to   *acabar*
fire   *la lumbre*
fish   *el pescado*
fish, to   *pescar*
flame   *la llama*
floor   *el piso*
flower   *la flor*
foot   *el pie*
footstool   *la banqueta*
fork   *el tenedor*
fresh   *fresco (a)*
friend   *el amigo (a)*
from   *desde*
front   *delante*
fruit   *la fruta*
fry, to   *freír*

G

game   *el juego*
garbage   *los desperdicios de la casa*
garden   *el jardín*
gardener   *el jardinero*
garlic   *el ajo*
gelatin   *la gelatina*
gin   *la ginebra*
give, to   *dar*
glass   *el vaso*
go, to   *ir*
gold   *el oro*
good   *bueno (a)*
grandchildren   *los nietos*
grandparents   *los abuelos*
grape   *la uva*
grapefruit   *la toronja*
griddle   *el comal*

grocery   *la tienda de comestibles*

H

hair   *el pelo*
haircut   *el corte de pelo*
half   *medio*
hall   *el pasillo*
ham   *el jamón*
hamburger   *la hamburguesa*
hammer   *el martillo*
hand   *la mano*
handkerchief   *el pañuelo*
hanger   *el gancho*
happy   *feliz*
head   *la cabeza*
headache   *dolor de cabeza*
heater   *el calentador*
heavy   *pesado*
heel   *el talón*
help, to   *ayudar*
here   *aquí*
high   *alto (a)*
honey   *la miel*
hose   *la manguera*
hot   *caliente*
house   *la casa*
how   *cómo*
how much   *cuánto?*
hunger   *la hambre*
hurry, to   *apresurar (se)*
husband   *el esposo*

I

ice   *el hielo*
ice cream   *el helado*
ill   *enfermo (a)*
inside   *dentro*
iodine   *el yodo*
iron   *la plancha*

iron, to   *planchar*
ironing board   *la tabla de planchar*

J

jacket   *el saco*
jelly   *la jalea*
jewelry   *las alhajas*
juice   *el jugo*

K

kettle   *la caldera*
key   *la llave*
kiss, to   *besar*
kitchen   *la cocina*
knee   *la rodilla*
knife   *el cuchillo*
know, to   *saber*

L

ladder   *la escalera*
lamb   *el cordero*
lamp   *la lámpara*
lampshade   *la pantalla*
latch   *la aldaba*
laundry   *la lavandería*
lawnmower   *la cortadora*
laxative   *el laxante*
leather   *el cuero*
left   *izquierdo (a)*
leg   *la pierna*
lemon   *el limón*
letter   *la carta*
lettuce   *la lechuga*
lid   *la tapadera*
light   *la luz*
light, to   *encender*
linen   *el lino*
lipstick   *el lápiz de labios*
liver   *el hígado*

lock up, to *encerrar*
look, to *mirar*
look for, to *buscar*
loud *alto*
love, to *amar*

M

magazine *la revista*
mail *la correspondencia*
man *el hombre*
matches *los fósforos*
mattress *el colchón*
measure, to *medir*
meat *la carne*
medicine *la medicina*
melon *el melón*
milk *la leche*
mirror *el espejo*
mix, to *mezclar*
money *el dinero*
mop *la aljofifa; el trapeador*
morning *la mañana*
mother *la madre*
mother-in-law *la suegra*
mouth *la boca*
mushroom *el hongo*

N

napkin *la servilleta*
near *cerca*
neck *el cuello*
need, to *necesitar*
needle *la aguja*
neighbor *el vecino (a)*
nephew *el sobrino*
never *nunca*
new *nuevo (a)*
newspaper *el diario; el periódico*
niece *la sobrina*

night *la noche*
nobody *nadie*
noise *el ruido*
noon *el mediodía*
nose *la nariz*
now *ahora*
nut *la nuez*
nutmeg *la nuez moscada*

O

oil *el aceite*
old *viejo (a)*
olives *las aceitunas*
onion *la cebolla*
open, to *abrir*
orange *la naranja*
other *otro (a)*
out *fuera*
oven *el horno*
overcoat *el sobretodo*
oyster *el ostión*

P

pail *el balde*
pan *el sartén*
pants *los pantalones*
paper *el papel*
parsley *el perejil*
peach *el durazno*
peanut *el cacahuate*
pear *la pera*
peas *los chícharos*
peel, to *pelar*
pen *la pluma*
pepper *la pimienta*
picture *el retrato*
pie *el pastel*
piece *el pedazo*
pillow *la almohada*
pillowcase *la funda*

pin   *la alfiler*
pineapple   *la piña*
plate   *el plato*
play, to   *jugar*
pliers   *las pinzas*
poison   *el veneno*
poor   *pobre*
pork   *el puerco*
pot   *el sartén*
potato   *la papa*
pound   *la libra*
powder   *el polvo*
pretty   *bonito (a)*
prune   *la ciruela*
purse   *la bolsa*
put, to   *colocar*

Q

quarter   *el cuarto*
quickly   *pronto*

R

radish   *el rábano*
rag   *la garra*
railroad   *el ferrocarril*
rain   *la lluvia*
raincoat   *el impermeable*
raisin   *la pasa*
raspberry   *la frambuesa*
rattle   *la sonaja*
raw   *crudo (a)*
red   *rojo (a)*
refrigerator   *el refrigerador*
remember, to   *acordase de*
rest, to   *descansar (se)*
rib   *la costilla*
ribbon   *el listón*
rich   *rico (a)*
right   *derecho (a)*
ring   *el anillo*

rinse, to   *enjuagar*
room   *el cuarto*
rotten   *podrido (a)*
round   *redondo (a)*
rubber   *el hule*
ruffle   *el olán*
rug, small   *el tapete*
rum   *el ron*

S

safety pin   *el seguro*
salad   *la ensalada*
sale   *la venta*
salt   *la sal*
sandwich   *el bocadillo*
sauce   *la salsa*
sausage   *el chorizo*
school   *la escuela*
scissors   *las tijeras*
scrambled   *revuelto*
screwdriver   *el desarmador*
seed   *la semilla*
servant   *la criada*
sew, to   *coser*
sewing machine   *la máquina*
shake, to   *sacudir*
sheet   *la sábana*
shirt   *la camisa*
shoe   *el zapato*
short   *corto (a)*
shrimp   *el camarón*
sick   *enfermo*
side   *el lado*
sifter   *el cernidor*
silk   *la seda*
silver   *la plata*
sink   *el albañal*
size   *el tamaño*
skillet   *el sartén*
slacks   *los pantalones*

sleep, to *dormir*
sleeve *la manga*
slow *lento (a)*
slowly *despacio*
smell *el olor*
smoke *el humo*
smoke, to *fumar*
soap *el jabón*
soft *blando (a)*
some *alguno (a)*
something *algo*
son *el hijo*
son-in-law *el yerno*
soon *pronto*
spice *la especie*
spinach *las espinacas*
sponge *la esponga*
spoon *la cuchara*
sprinkle, to *rociar*
squash *la calabaza*
stairway *la escalera*
starch *el almidón*
starch, to *almidonar*
steak *el bistec*
steam *el vapor*
stocking *la media*
stomach *el estómago*
stopper *el tapón*
stove *la estufa*
straight *derecho*
strainer *el colador*
strawberry *la fresa*
street *la calle*
sugar *la azúcar*
suit *el traje*
suitcase *la maleta*
sweep, to *barrer*
sweeper *la escoba mecánica*
swim, to *nadar*
syrup *el almíbar*

T

table *la mesa*
take, to *tomar*
taste, to *probar*
tea *el té*
tears *las lágrimas*
tender *blando (a)*
there *allá*
thimble *el dedal*
thing *la cosa*
thirst *la sed*
thread *el hilo*
throat *la garganta*
toast *el pan tostado*
toaster *el tostador*
toilet *el escusado*
toothache *dolor de muelas*
tomato *el tomate*
tongue *la lengua*
tonsils *las anginas*
torn *roto*
towel *la toalia*
toy *el juguete*
trash *la basura*
travel, to *caminar*
tree *el árbol*
trousers *los pantalones*
tub *la tina*
turkey *el cócono*
turnip *el nabo*
tweezers *las pinzas*

U

umbrella *el paraguas*
under *debajo (de)*
underneath *bajo*
understand, to *comprender*
underwear *la ropa íntima*

up   *arriba*
use, to   *emplear*

V

vacuum cleaner   *la aspiradora*
vanilla   *la vainilla*
vase   *el florero*
veal   *la ternera (o)*
venetian blinds   *las persianas*
very   *muy*
view   *la vista*
vinegar   *el vinagre*
vitamin   *la vitamina*
voice   *la voz*

W

wait, to   *esperar*
walk, to   *andar*
wall   *la pared*
wallet   *la cartera*
wash, to   *lavar*
washbasin   *el lavamanos*
washer   *la lavadora*
washing machine   *la máquina para lavar*
waste, to   *gastar*
watch   *el reloj*
water   *la agua*

watermelon   *la sandía*
wax   *la cera*
weather   *el tiempo*
wedding   *la boda*
week   *la semana*
welcome   *bienvenido (a)*
well   *bien*
wet   *mojado*
when   *cuándo*
where   *dónde*
while   *mientras*
whiskey   *el aguardiente*
why   *porqué*
wide   *ancho (a)*
wife   *la esposa*
window   *la ventana*
wine   *el vino*
with   *con*
woman   *la mujer*
wool   *la lana*
work   *el trabajo*
wringer   *el exprimidor*
wrist   *la muñeca*
wrong side out   *al revés*

Y

yellow   *amarillo (a)*
yesterday   *ayer*
young   *joven*